SUPPLEMENTARY STUDIES
for Clarinet
By
R. M. ENDRESEN

PREFACE

The important features of the SUPPLEMENTARY STUDIES for Clarinet may be summed up as follows:

1. They are tuneful.

2. Their construction makes for a more accurate technique. (Notice how fast passages are confined to small groups, allowing the student to get his bearings without slowing up the tempo intended for the study.)

3. There are frequent sustained passages to develop tone and phrasing.

4. The high range is introduced in a progressive manner, (half and quarter notes) permitting the student to think of fingerings with a minimum of confusion.

5. They are really progressive foundation material. While only the common key signatures have been used, practically all the flats and sharps are touched upon in chromatic passages.

6. They will prove useful as review work for more advanced students.

7. May be used to correct poor reading or inaccurate rhythm, when too difficult material has been resorted to.

8. Their length prohibits boredom.

    I find that my most advanced students enjoy playing the studies, as well as grade school pupils.

R. M. Endresen

SUPPLEMENTARY STUDIES
for Clarinet
To be used with, or to follow any method.

R. M. ENDRESEN

Copyright MCMXXXIV by Rubank Inc.
International Copyright Secured

S.S. for Clar. 24 *Note: Fingerings indicated are for Boehm System Clarinet. K = Key. L = Left Hand. R = Right Hand.

4

5

6

7

Andante

8

March time

9

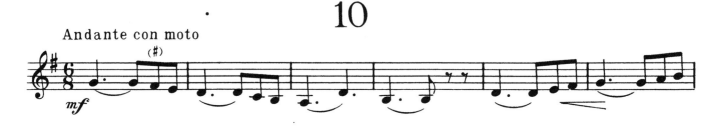

10

Andante con moto

11

Allegro

12

Largo

13

14

15

16

In strict rhythm

17

Allegro

18

19

S. S. for Clar. 24

20

Allegretto

21

Allegro

D.C.

22

March time

23

Moderato

24

Andante sostenuto

Animato

25

Andante

26

Staccatto

S.S.for Clar. 24

27

28

29

Allegro moderato

30

Scherzando

31

Andante

32

Moderato

33

Animato

34

Moderato

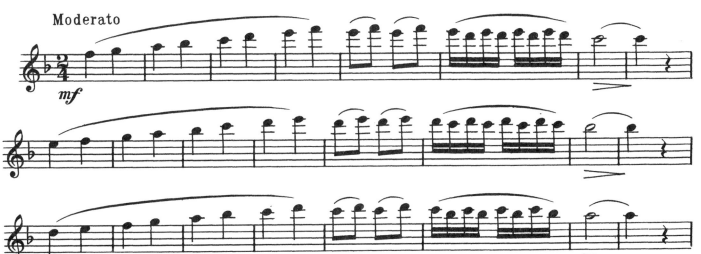

35

Allegretto

36

Moderato

37